OPERA LIBRETTI

English Versions by EDWARD J. DENT

THE BARBER OF SEVILLE

DON GIOVANNI

FIDELIO

THE MAGIC FLUTE

THE MARRIAGE OF FIGARO

MARTHA

ORPHEUS

RIGOLETTO

LA TRAVIATA

IL TROVATORE

Price 2s. 6d. net each

Other operas in preparation

THE MAGIC FLUTE

(*Die Zauberflote*)

AN OPERA IN TWO ACTS

Words by
CARL LUDWIG GIESECKE
and
EMANUEL SCHIKANEDER

Music by
WOLFGANG AMADEUS MOZART

English Version by
EDWARD J. DENT

OXFORD UNIVERSITY PRESS
LONDON   NEW YORK   TORONTO

NOTE

All applications for permission to use the English text here printed should be addressed to the Publisher

———

Acknowledgement is due to Miss Lilian Baylis and Mr. Owen P. Smyth for permission to reproduce the illustration of Sadler's Wells Theatre which appears on the cover

First published . 1937
Reprinted . . 1943

PRINTED IN GREAT BRITAIN

PREFACE

WHEN the first of all operas was produced at Florence towards the end of the sixteenth century (the date is uncertain) the book of words was printed (in 1600) probably as a souvenir to be given away to the noble ladies and gentlemen who had been invited to the performance, and ever since then it has been the custom to print the words of operas as little books—hence the international name for it, *libretto*, a little book. The first librettos were written by real poets; in fact the words were often better than the music. As long as operas were composed mainly for the cultivated classes, librettos maintained a reasonably high standard, in whatever language they were written. Quinault wrote in French for Lully, Dryden for Purcell in the seventeenth century; in Italy Apostolo Zeno and Metastasio carried on the tradition of literary dignity into the eighteenth. That century, too, is the great age of comic opera, with admirable humorists such as Goldoni, Bickerstaffe, Sedaine, and Casti—the Gilbert of his day—to say nothing of Mozart's friend Da Ponte. It was not until the days of Verdi—from about 1840 onwards—that the word *libretto* became a byword for nonsense and doggerel. Verdi's audiences were noisy and ill-educated; they wanted roaring melodrama (the word *melodramma* is the classical Italian word for *opera,* which about 1650 was still rather colloquial), with music that could be taken up for political purposes. No wonder that there are still nice-minded people who say they prefer their operas in a language they do not understand.

Opera in English dates back to 1656, but after the death of Purcell in 1695, it languished. Italian opera was established as a fashionable entertainment, and opera in English was only what we should call 'musical comedy'. Out of this comic opera grew what in the nineteenth century was known as 'grand romantic opera'; and its English landmarks were Weber's *Oberon*, written for London, 1826, and the English performances of Beethoven's *Fidelio* (with Malibran as the heroine) in 1833. But it is difficult to translate bad Italian into anything but worse English, and the result has been that opera in English is to most people a lamentably ridiculous affair. Opera in English will never flourish until a tradition of really good translation is established. Far be it from me to speak ill of my predecessors: Thomas Oliphant's version of *Fidelio* (1833) is a model of good style. Unfortunately it sounds too elegant for the present day; owing to changes in literary convention translations, like accompaniments to folksongs, must sooner or later become out of date, and have to be rewritten.

English is a perfectly good language for singing, if singers will take the trouble to pronounce it naturally, as actors do. Even when English is difficult to sing, it is less difficult than German can be in some of the standard German operas. The first duty of a translator is to make the story of the opera clear, and to write words simple enough to be intelligible when sung. If only for this reason, the words must be accurately fitted to the music; and after all these conditions are fulfilled, there is not much chance left for 'poetry'. The reader is asked to remember that the words of these English versions have been written to be sung and acted, not to be read. Stage scenery is not meant to be hung in a private house; the scene-painter is satisfied if it looks reasonably well on the stage. If the reader discovers in these pages any line that he can call poetry, he may be sure that it has been stolen from some more respectable—and, I hope, non-copyright —author.

E. J. D.

Autumn, 1937

INTRODUCTION

LIFE OF MOZART

WOLFGANG AMADEUS MOZART was born on January 27, 1756, at Salzburg, in Austria, where his father, the son of a bookbinder at Augsburg, was a musician in the service of the Archbishop. Wolfgang's talents developed very early, and his father exhibited him as an infant prodigy at Vienna and Paris, in London and in Italy. During his boyhood he composed several operas, which are now forgotten; his first really important work for the stage was *Idomeneo*, written at the age of 25. This was a tragic opera in the old Italian style, and was produced at Munich. It is occasionally given in Germany, and contains much beautiful music, but its profoundly serious character has prevented it from becoming popular. In 1782 Mozart married and settled at Vienna, where he produced *Die Entführung aus dem Serail* (known in England as *Il Seraglio*), a German light opera, in the same year, and in 1786 the Italian comic opera *Le Nozze di Figaro*. Two more Italian comic operas followed—*Don Giovanni* (Prague, 1788) and *Così fan tutte* (Vienna, 1790). In 1791 he composed *La Clemenza di Tito*, a formal Italian opera for the coronation of the Emperor Leopold at Prague, and (in German) *The Magic Flute*, produced at Vienna on September 30. On December 5 Mozart died, having not quite completed his thirty-sixth year.

THE MAGIC FLUTE

The last two years of his life had been full of misfortune. His best patron, the Emperor Joseph II, died in the early part of 1790, and Mozart was not in favour with his successor. His compositions brought him no profits; his pupils had dwindled to two. His wife suffered from chronic illness, and his own health had been seriously undermined. He was a bad man of business, always ready to help a needy friend, and careless about his own affairs. In the spring of 1791 his old friend the actor-manager Schikaneder suggested that he should write music for a fairy play to be performed at his theatre, a mere wooden booth set up in a courtyard in the outskirts of Vienna. It was a strange commission for a man who had been court-composer to accept, but Mozart accepted it, though feeling very diffident of success. The book had been put together by a chorus singer named Giesecke, and Schikaneder had added a large comic part (Papageno) for himself. Giesecke afterwards left the stage and devoted himself to science. He travelled in Greenland for seven years, and in 1813 became Professor of Mineralogy at Dublin, where he died in 1833.

The plot of the opera suffered from being altered in the course of composition, but in its final form it may be summarized as follows:

Story of the Opera

Act I. Tamino, an Egyptian prince, being pursued by a monstrous serpent, is rescued by three Ladies in attendance on the Queen of Night. They present him with the portrait of Pamina, the Queen's daughter, with whom he instantly falls in love, and send him to rescue her from the clutches of Sarastro, whom they depict as an evil magician. To protect him on his journey they give him a magic flute; the bird-catcher, Papageno, who is sent with him, is provided with a chime of magic bells. Papageno arrives first at Sarastro's palace (Scene II), and having frightened away the negro Monostatos, who was about to assault Pamina, persuades her to attempt an escape. Tamino (Scene III) is led up to the temple by three Genii, who warn him mysteriously to be 'silent, patient, persevering'. Full of youthful enthusiasm, he attempts to make his entrance, but after being twice repulsed is met on the threshold by a priest (the Orator), who tells him that he has been deceived by the Queen and her Ladies as to the real character of Sarastro, and that he will only understand the truth

> 'When friendship leads thee by the hand
> To join the temple's sacred band.'

His old ideals are shattered, but the music of the magic flute soothes his agitation, and mysterious voices tell him that Pamina is still alive.

Meanwhile Pamina and Papageno have escaped from Monostatos by means of the magic bells, but are cut off by the arrival of Sarastro himself. Pamina confesses her attempt at flight; Sarastro, with characteristic gentleness, bids her be patient. Monostatos having caught Tamino brings him to Sarastro, but instead of seeing him punished is punished himself. The first Act ends with Tamino and Papageno being led into the temple to prepare for initiation into the mysteries of Osiris and Isis.

Act II. Sarastro and the Priests having agreed (Scene I) to accept Tamino as a candidate for initiation, Tamino and Papageno are submitted to various ordeals. They successfully resist the attempt of the three Ladies (Scene II) to make them abandon the idea of being initiated. In Scene III Monostatos makes another assault upon Pamina, but is frustrated by the Queen, who gives Pamina a dagger and bids her kill Sarastro. Scene IV brings the second ordeal: Pamina reproaches Tamino for having ceased to love her, while Tamino is obliged to listen to her in silence, and in Scene V takes farewell of her in the presence of Sarastro and the Priests. She attempts to commit suicide, but is prevented by the Three Genii (Scene VII), and in Scene VIII passes through the final tests of fire and water with Tamino. Scenes VI and IX are taken up with comic love-scenes between Papageno and an old woman, who is eventually transformed into a girl. The final scene shows the Queen and her Ladies, guided by Monostatos, making a last desperate attempt to break into the temple; on the appearance of Sarastro they vanish into the darkness, and the opera ends with a chorus in praise of the lovers and their courageous devotion.

THE HIDDEN MEANING OF THE STORY

One of the reasons which led to the extraordinary success of *The Magic Flute* was that underneath this apparently foolish fairy-story there were concealed allusions to the rites and doctrines of Freemasonry. Towards the end of the eighteenth century Freemasonry had become very widespread on the Continent, largely because the idealism of its teaching and the secrecy of its methods were valuable aids to the propagation of humanitarian principles. It must be remembered that in 1791 such ideas as that of 'Liberty, Equality, and Fraternity' had not been accepted freely by continental governments, least of all in Austria, in spite of the liberal tendencies of Joseph II. Giesecke, Schikaneder, and Mozart were all enthusiastic Freemasons, and so were most of the eminent men of the period, including Voltaire, Goethe, and Haydn. For the audience which listened to *The Magic Flute* in 1791,

Sarastro and the Priests of Isis represented the Free-masons, the Queen of Night the Empress Maria Theresa, and Monostatos the clerical party, who were the sworn enemies of the new ideas.

To a modern English audience the opera naturally appeals first and foremost by the beauty of its music. But it must not be forgotten that Mozart (as is clear from his letters to his wife) wished the opera to be taken seriously, and was annoyed when people regarded it merely as a piece of buffoonery. It is not necessary to be a Freemason to appreciate the allegory. Tamino, the hero, is Everyman; first we see him educated by the Three Ladies, who represent conventionalism, then, at the gate of the temple suddenly forced to think for himself, instead of accepting what they have taught him. Sarastro and the priests open his eyes to a new ideal, the life of reason, and a religion of love and brotherhood. Pamina, his chosen bride, has had to endure the tyranny of Monostatos, who represents unreasoning authority; but she escapes and, together with Tamino, passes through the fire and water, symbolizing the trials and sorrows of a lifetime, until both are finally received into the company of the enlightened.

CHARACTERS

(in the order of their appearance)

TAMINO, an Egyptian Prince.

THREE LADIES in attendance on the Queen of Night.

PAPAGENO, a bird-catcher.

THE QUEEN OF NIGHT.

MONOSTATOS, a Moor in the service of Sarastro.

PAMINA, daughter of the Queen of Night.

THREE GENII.

A PRIEST (the Orator).

SARASTRO, High Priest of Osiris and Isis.

SECOND PRIEST.

AN OLD WOMAN (afterwards PAPAGENA).

TWO MEN IN ARMOUR.

SLAVES, PRIESTS, PEOPLE, ETC.

*The scene is laid in Egypt in the neighbourhood of
a temple of Osiris and Isis.*

First performance, Vienna, 30 September 1791.

*First performance in Paris (much distorted and mutilated as
'Les Mystères d'Isis') 20 August 1801.*

*First performances in London, King's Theatre, 6 June 1811
(in Italian); Covent Garden, 27 May 1833 (in German);
Drury Lane, 10 March 1838 (in English).*

First performance in English, New York, 17 April 1833.

*First performance of this English version, New Theatre,
Cambridge, 1 December 1911.*

I pray you all give your audience,
And hear this matter with reverence,
     By figure a moral play.

EVERYMAN.

ACT I

Scene I

TAMINO rushes on, carrying a bow, but no arrows.
He is pursued by a huge serpent.

No. 1. Introduction

TAMINO

Oh help me! protect me! will no one stand by me?
Deserted in danger, oh where shall I fly me?
The poisonous fangs of the serpent are on me—
O gods, now have mercy!
See, nearer it draws
With white cruel jaws!
Too late it is, I cannot fly—
Ye gods protect me, or I die!

He falls, exhausted.

Three Ladies enter, carrying spears, and kill the serpent.

3 LADIES. Back, loathly worm, to Hell and die!
'Tis ours alone the victory.
To save this youth in danger's hour
'Twas only virtue had the power.

1ST LADY. How comely is this youth and fair!

2ND LADY. How sweet, how gracious is his air!

3RD LADY. No art could paint a face so rare!

3 LADIES. Ah, were I not to virtue bound,
My heart its choice in him had found.
Then to the Queen our footsteps winging,
Let us this joyful news be bringing;
Perchance to her unending grief
This noble youth may bear relief.

1ST LADY.   Then haste at once away,
And I with him will stay.

2ND LADY.   For you to go 'twere best,
And I will guard his rest.

3RD LADY.   Nay, you must go, 'tis plain,
And I will here remain.

1ST LADY.   Nay, I with him will stay.

2ND LADY.   Nay, I will guard his rest.

3RD LADY.   Nay, I will here remain.

3 LADIES.   I'll guard him, I, I, I!
What! must I go?
Not I, no, no!
Since each alone with him would stay,
Of course she finds us in the way.

I can contain myself no longer;
My passion fiercer grows and stronger;
Could I but be with him alone!
Yet neither moves; they stand like stone.
My only course is to be gone.

Farewell, farewell, my heart's own joy!
Farewell, farewell, entrancing boy!
My heart will aye be sore
To see thy face once more.

Exeunt Ladies.

TAM.   Where am I?—The serpent, dead at my feet!

A pan-pipe is heard off the stage.

Ha! is that a man coming?

Retires.

PAPAGENO *enters singing.*

No. 2. Song

PAPAGENO

Now tell me, did you ever see
So queer a kind of man as me?
Yet young and old in every place
Are always glad to see my face.
I spread my nets and whistle clear
To catch the birds as they come near,
And from this cage they cannot stir,
For I'm the jolly bird-catcher.

But there's a sport that's finer yet
Than traps for silly birds to set;
Yes, braver game there is, I know,
And after it I mean to go.
I'd gladly ply the fowler's trade
If I could catch a pretty maid.
Then who would share the cage with her?
Why, sure, the jolly bird-catcher!

TAM. You merry fellow, tell me, who are you?

PAP. Who am I? why, a man like yourself, of course.
And who are you?

TAM. I am the Prince Tamino.

PAP. Prince? What's that?

TAM. My father is a King and rules over wide lands and
much people; that is why I am called a Prince.

PAP. Lands? people? a prince? Tell me then, are there
other lands and other people beyond those hills?

TAM. Yes, thousands and thousands.

3

PAP. Then perhaps I might go and sell my birds there.

TAM. But tell me, what is this country? Who is king over it?

PAP. I don't know.

TAM. Where do you come from?

PAP. I don't know.

TAM. How do you live, then?

PAP. By eating and drinking, of course, like any one else. I catch birds for the Queen of Night and her ladies, who give me food and drink in exchange.

TAM. The Queen of Night?

PAP. (*aside*). How he stares at me! I'm quite frightened. (*To* TAMINO.) Why do you look at me like that?

TAM. Well, I'm not so sure that you are a man after all.

PAP. Not a man? why not?

TAM. With all those feathers, you look more like—

PAP. Like one of my own birds? Have a care what you say. I have a giant's strength! (*Aside*.) If that does not frighten him away, I shall have to run away myself.

TAM. Then perhaps it was you that killed the serpent, and saved my life?

PAP. What serpent? (*Sees the serpent and starts*.) Oh! is it alive?

TAM. How did you kill it? You have no weapons.

PAP. What should I want with weapons?

Shows his arms.

TAM. You throttled it?

PAP. Of course I throttled it. (*Aside*.) I never knew I was so strong.

4

Enter the Three Ladies, veiled.

LADIES (*all together*). Papageno!

PAP. Ha! That's meant for me. (*To* TAMINO.) Look there, friend!

TAM. Who are those ladies?

PAP. I don't know. They take my birds every day, and give me wine, bread, and fruit in exchange for them.

TAM. They must surely be very beautiful.

PAP. No, no, if they were beautiful, they wouldn't hide their faces.

LADIES. Papageno!

PAP. Beautiful? I never saw anything lovelier in my life. (*Aside.*) That will please them.

LADIES. Papageno!

PAP. (*aside*). What have I done to make them so angry? (*To the ladies.*) Fair ladies, here are your birds.

1ST LADY. No wine for you to-day, Papageno—only cold water.

2ND LADY. No bread for you to-day, Papageno—only a stone.

3RD LADY. No fruit for you to-day, Papageno—you are to have your mouth locked up with this padlock.

She locks up his mouth.

1ST LADY. Do you wish to know why the Queen has ordered you to be punished in this way?

PAPAGENO nods.

2ND LADY. So that you may tell no more lies to strangers.

3RD LADY. Tell us, did you kill the serpent?

PAPAGENO shakes his head.

2ND LADY. Who did, then?

          PAPAGENO *signifies that he does not know.*

IST LADY. Prince, it was we who saved you. Our mistress, the Queen of Night, sends you this portrait of her daughter. Should the sight of those features leave you not utterly indifferent, there awaits you a great and glorious future. We meet again!

        Exeunt Three Ladies, followed by PAPAGENO.

No. 3. ARIA

TAMINO

O loveliness beyond compare!
Was ever maiden half so fair?
I know not if 'tis joy or pain
That overwhelms my reeling brain.

I know not what is this emotion
That fires my heart with strange devotion;
Can it be love that leads me on?
Ah yes, it must be love alone.

Oh could I only kneel before her?
Tell her how madly I adore her!
And fearing, hoping—maid divine!
Ah, what would I?—

Within these arms I would enfold her,
To this my burning heart fast hold her,
And so for ever were she mine.

Re-enter the Three Ladies.

IST LADY. Prince, the Queen has heard your every word—

2ND LADY. She has read your every look—

3RD LADY. She has resolved to make you the happiest man on earth. If you are as chivalrous as you are passionate, it will be your privilege to effect the rescue of her most unhappy daughter, Pamina.

TAM. Pamina! Pamina unhappy?

1ST LADY. Yes, alas! an evil magician has carried her off, and holds her in durance vile.

TAM. His name!

2ND LADY. Sarastro!

3RD LADY. The high priest of the Sun.

TAM. Pamina a prisoner in his hands? Ladies, by the fire that burns within me, I swear to be her deliverer. Lead on!

1ST LADY. Brave youth!   *Thunder.*

2ND LADY. She comes!   *Thunder.*

3RD LADY. The Queen!

> *Thunder. It grows dark. The* QUEEN OF NIGHT *appears.*

No. 4. RECITATIVE AND ARIA

QUEEN OF NIGHT

Recit. Be not afraid, O noble youth,
    I know thy virtue, courage, truth;
    To thee alone can turn in desolation
    The Queen of highest Heaven for consolation.

Aria. All joy from me has now departed;
    How can I e'er forget that day
    Which from her mother broken-hearted
    My daughter all unwilling parted?
    My bitterest foe snatch'd her away.

What horror came o'er me! my prayers unavailing,
I heard her protesting, beseeching, bewailing;
Before my eyes I saw him seize her—
'O help!' can I forget that cry?
Not all my tears could e'er release her,
Against his craft no power had I.

Thou, Prince, with manly ardour burnest,
Thou shalt to me my child restore;
And when victorious thou returnest,
I plight her thine for evermore.

> *The* QUEEN *disappears, and the Ladies follow her.*
> *It grows light again.*

TAM. Am I dreaming? (*Looks at portrait.*) No—it cannot be.

PAPAGENO *enters, pointing to his mouth and trying to speak.*

No. 5. QUINTET

PAP.   Hm hm hm hm hm hm hm hm!
              Hm hm hm hm hm hm hm!

TAM.   'Tis hard such punishment to suffer;
              Thy lips are tight lock'd up, I see;
              To loose thy bonds I'd gladly offer,
              But have no power to set thee free.

> *Enter the Three Ladies.*

1ST LADY. Our gracious Queen her pardon sends,
              If thou wilt strive to make amends.

> *She removes the padlock from* PAPAGENO's *mouth.*

PAP.   Oh joy, once more I'm free to chatter!

2ND LADY. Remember, 'tis no laughing matter!

PAP.   No lie shall pass my lips again;
              I'll ne'er forget that padlock's pain.

LADIES.   Thou'lt never forget that padlock's pain.

ALL.   If lying lips could all be fetter'd,
             And made secure with lock and key,
             Then falsehood's hateful might were shatter'd,
             And man with man at peace could be.
                        The 1ST LADY *hands* TAMINO *a flute.*

1ST LADY.   O Prince, our Queen this gift bestows,
             Since thy devotion well she knows:
             She deigns the magic flute to send thee;
             In every peril 'twill defend thee.

3 LADIES.   Unbounded power to him is granted
             Who sounds aright its notes enchanted;
             The deepest grief to joy 'twill turn,
             Make hardest heart with love to burn.

ALL.   Yes, 'tis only music
             That has the power to weave that spell,
             Jarring souls so to attune
             That all in harmony may dwell.

PAP.   Ladies fair, with your permission,
             May I take my leave of you?

LADIES.   Nay, but hear this new commission
             That the Queen would have thee do;
             With the Prince she'd have thee faring,
             All his dangers with him sharing—

PAP.   Face Sarastro? No, not I!
             You yourselves to me have sworn,
             If to enter I should try,
             Where his savage guards are posted,
             He would have me pluck'd and roasted,
             Or by dogs to pieces torn.

9

LADIES.	Nay, on the Prince alone rely, No harm can come while he is nigh.
PAP.	Rely on him? the Devil take him! My life too dear I hold: He'll run away, or I mistake him, 'Twill be just as I foretold.
1ST LADY.	See what the Queen has sent for thee. *She hands* PAPAGENO *a chime of bells.*
PAP.	Aha! whatever can it be?
LADIES.	A peal of bells with magic jingle.
PAP.	To make them ring my fingers tingle.
LADIES.	Then ring amain and merry be.
ALL.	Flute for music, bells for laughter, Best of comrades now or after! Trust them well, they bear a charm Safe to keep you both from harm.
TAM.	But, ladies, I entreat you, say—
PAP.	What road to take, how find the way?
LADIES.	Three gentle spirits shall protect you, And in the way of truth direct you; Their counsel they will lend at need, Only to them shall you give heed. So may you soon your end attain, Farewell! farewell! we meet again.

Scene II

MONOSTATOS *drags on* PAMINA.

No. 6. Terzetto

MON.	My pretty maid, I hold thee fast!
PAM.	This hour will surely be my last.

MON.   I'll take no more denying.

PAM.   I'll die before complying.
        Oh, were my mother only near,
        'Twould break her heart thy words to hear.

MONOSTATOS claps his hands. Enter Slaves.

MON.   Bring chains and make her hands secure!
        I'll force thee to obey me.
                    The Slaves chain PAMINA.

PAM.   Oh slay me, rather slay me!
        Or must I worse than death endure?
                 She sinks unconscious.

MON.   She's mine at last! Now is my conquest sure.

MONOSTATOS signs to the Slaves to depart. PAPA-
GENO *puts his head in.*

PAP.   What place is this? where have I strayed?
        Just now I heard a clatter;
        Well, well, I'm not afraid.   *He enters.*
        Good morrow, pretty maid;
           Come, tell me what's the matter?—

MONOSTATOS and PAPAGENO *catch sight of each
other simultaneously; each is terrified at the other.*

MON. }   That is the Devil certainly!
PAP. }   Have mercy! oh! he's come for me!

MONOSTATOS and PAPAGENO *run off in opposite
directions;* PAMINA *recovers herself.*

PAM. Mother! Mother! Oh, shall I never escape that
cruel Moor?

PAP. (*re-entering*). What a fool I was to be frightened!
I've seen plenty of black birds in my life, so why

shouldn't there be black men too? (*Sees* PAMINA.) Ah! there's the pretty maid still. (*To* PAMINA.) Are you the daughter of the Queen of Night?

PAM. Yes.

PAP. Then I have news for you. The Queen has sent me——

PAM. (*eagerly*). My mother sent you? But who are you? What is your name?

PAP. Papageno.

PAM. Papageno? Papageno? Yes, I remember I used to hear about you, though I never saw you.

PAP. I'm her Majesty's bird-catcher! I was bringing my birds to the palace early this morning, when I met a strange young man who calls himself a prince. Your mother took a great fancy to him, gave him your portrait, and told him to go and rescue you. As soon as he set eyes on the portrait, he fell in love with you, and swore he would never rest till he had found you.

PAM. He fell in love with me?

PAP. We set out at once, and here we are.

PAM. But when Sarastro comes back and finds you here——

PAP. He's out? Then there's not a moment to lose. Come, let's run away at once, and find the young prince.

PAM. The young prince! He—fell in love with me, you said?

PAP. Yes—and I believe you've fallen in love with him without seeing even so much as his portrait. And nobody ever falls in love with me.

PAM. Poor Papageno! You must be very unhappy!

PAP. I should think I was! If I can't find a wife I shall pluck out all my feathers one by one and then die.

PAM. No, no, Papageno; take heart—I'm sure every one finds somebody to love them sooner or later.

No. 7. Duet

PAM. The kindly voice of Mother Nature
Wakes love in bird and beast and flower;

PAP. There's not on earth a single creature
That can resist that tender power.

BOTH. The law of love let us then own,
All life depends on love alone.

PAM. That joy to every creature granted
Is felt no less by all mankind;

PAP. 'Tis deep in every soul implanted
That each its kindred soul must find.

BOTH. The law of love let us then own,
All life depends on love alone.
They that know the joys of love
Rise to join the gods above.

Scene III

Tamino is led on by the Three Genii.

No. 8. Finale

3 GEN. Thus far we set thee on thy way;
Fare forth alone, no danger fearing.
Yet ever this command obey:
Be silent, patient, persevering!

TAM. Oh tell me, tell me, spirits three,
If I may set Pamina free?

3 GEN.   Such words are not for us to say;
              Be silent, patient, persevering!
              A manly part thou hast to play,
              If this the goal thou would'st be nearing.

                                                  Exeunt.

TAM.   Oh may these mystic words of wisdom
              Upon my heart be grav'd for ever.
              What is my fate? where am I now?
              O surely, none but gods dwell here.
              What words do I read there inscrib'd on the
                    gateway?
              'To Nature, to Reason, to Wisdom, these temples.'
              But who were the builders that rais'd them so fair?
              Ah, sure nothing evil could find harbour there.
              Then scorning all danger an entrance I'll make;
              My purpose is noble, my honour's at stake!
              Thou vile seducer, tremble now!
              To save Pamina was my vow.

                    He moves towards the right-hand entrance.

VOICES (*behind*). Stand back!

TAM. Stand back? I'll try my fortune here.

                    He moves towards the left-hand entrance.

VOICES (*behind*). Stand back!

TAM.   What? here too I'm repuls'd?
              But yet, one door there still remains;
              Perchance I'll find an entrance there.

    *He is about to go up to the central door. A priest
    (the Orator) comes out of the temple.*

PRIEST. What wouldst thou here, audacious youth?
                  What seek'st in this our sanctuary?

TAM.   I come by right of Love and Truth.

PRIEST. Thy words ring noble to the ear;
    But say, what right hast thou to speak them?
    Not Love nor Truth thy passion guides,
    But Lies and Hatred sent thee hither.

TAM. Yes, hatred for a cruel deed.

PRIEST. We know no act or thought that's cruel.

TAM. This is the stronghold of Sarastro.

PRIEST. 'Tis true, Sarastro rules us here.

TAM. Yet not in Wisdom's holy shrine?

PRIEST. Of all her sons the wisest he.

TAM. Your wisdom's nought but vile deceit!

PRIEST. Wilt thou so soon be gone?

TAM. Yes, let me go; hateful place!
    Why did I e'er come here!

PRIEST. Nay, tell me all thy mind; methinks thou art
    deceiv'd.

TAM. Sarastro rules you here; that surely is enough.

PRIEST. If life be dear to thee, speak further, go not hence.
    Sarastro dost thou hate?

TAM. There's none that I hate more.

PRIEST. Why dost thou hate him? Tell me that.

TAM. Is he not cruel past belief?

PRIEST. What proof is there of that thou sayest?

TAM. A woman's tears may surely prove it,
    Whom he has plung'd in endless woe.

PRIEST. A woman then has told thee this?
    'Twas like a woman thus to talk,
    And like a boy to think it true.
    Wait till Sarastro show to thee
    The purpose of his action here.

TAM.   His purpose is but all too clear:
          Did he not snatch the fair Pamina
          By force from her unhappy mother?

PRIEST.   Yes, surely, that I'll not deny.

TAM.   Where is she? or am I too late?
          Was hers some doom I dare not name?

PRIEST.   My son, have patience, wait a while;
          'Tis yet too soon to answer thee.

TAM.   What means this riddle? speak the truth.

PRIEST.   My tongue is bound by duty's oath.

TAM.   When wilt thou break the bond of silence?

PRIEST.   When friendship leads thee by the hand
          To join the temple's holy band.
                              He goes back into the temple.

TAM.   O endless night! hast thou no breaking?
          When dawns the day mine eyes are seeking?

VOICES (*behind*). Soon, soon; courage, seek the light!

TAM.   Light! light! yes, though it blind mine eyes.
          O tell me, voice of mystery,
          Lives then Pamina still?

VOICES.   Pamina still doth live.

TAM.   She lives? I thank you for that word.
          Oh that my tongue could only utter,
          Ye gods above, my grateful rapture;
          Pamina lives! shall I not soon behold her?
          Yes, for her all I'll endure!
                              He takes his flute and plays.

          O voice of magic melody!
          O strain enthralling!
          Serener thoughts thou wak'st in me,
          My soul to loftier purpose calling.

Wild nature's children own thy charm,
And flock around, their haunts deserting:
The fierce lose all desire to harm,
The timid fear no hurting.

Ah, but Pamina's far away;
Pamina, hear me, hear me play!
In vain—where shall I find thee, say!

PAPAGENO's *pan-pipe is heard answering the flute.*

Ah! a familiar note I hear,
That tells me Papageno's near.
Perchance Pamina he has found,
Perchance she hears the magic sound,
Perchance the flute will guide my steps to her.

He rushes off; PAPAGENO *and* PAMINA *hurry on round the opposite corner.*

PAM.⎫ Let us hasten quick as thought,
PAP.⎭ To escape before we're caught;
If we once the Prince can find,
Then our danger's left behind.

PAM. Oh, Tamino!

PAP. Hush, be silent! I know better how to call him.

He whistles; the flute answers from behind.

BOTH. Yes, the magic flute gives answer,
Yes, again its notes I hear,
Then Tamino must be near!
'Twas the surest way to greet him;
Let us hasten on to meet him.

They run off, but are intercepted and driven back by MONOSTATOS.

C

MON.　Let us hasten on to meet him!
　　　Ha! caught in the very act!
　　　So you thought you could escape me!
　　　I'll teach you to disobey me!
　　　With Monostatos to trifle!
　　　Ne'er again shall you defy me!
　　　Come, ye slaves, and bind them fast.

PAM.⎫
PAP.⎭　All our fairest hopes are past.

MON.　Slaves, I say! come, bind them fast!
　　　　　　Enter slaves with chains.

PAP.　Just a chance I still can see;
　　　Here's the thing to set us free.
　　　Set the magic bells a-ringing;
　　　Help to us they may be bringing.

He plays on the bells. MONOSTATOS *and the slaves
are startled and drop the chains; they begin to sing,
and dance off grotesquely.*

MON.　⎰O listen, what is it that tinkles so clear?
SLAVES.⎱'Tis something I never did see or did hear.

PAM.⎫　When the magic bells are heard
PAP.⎭　　　Chimes of music waking,
　　　Wrath forgets his angry word,
　　　　　Frowns to smiles are breaking.
　　　Thus our foes to friends we turn;
　　　Thus to laugh we make them learn.

　　　Make them laugh and make them sing;
　　　　　Friendship follows after;
　　　So to every man we bring
　　　　　Music, friendship, laughter!

> *A flourish of trumpets. The Chorus are heard singing behind.*

CHORUS. All hail to Sarastro! we bend before him!

PAP. What means all that shouting? some danger
approaches!

PAM. Oh friend, no hope indeed remains;
It means that great Sarastro comes.

PAP. I wish I were a mouse,
Within some cranny hiding,
Or like a snail were sliding
Into my little house!
But say, what answer can we give him?

PAM. The truth, friend; ne'er would I deceive him.

> *Enter Priests and People, followed by* SARASTRO
> *and Attendants.*

CHORUS. All hail to Sarastro! we bend low before him,
With heartfelt devotion and love we adore him.
'Tis his loving wisdom that guides us aright;
Then lead us, Sarastro, to truth and to light!

> PAMINA *throws herself at* SARASTRO's *feet.*

PAM. Sir, let me all confess to thee:
I broke thy law and sought escape.
But yet not all the fault was mine;
The wicked Moor with love pursued me:
That was the cause for which I fled.

SAR. Arise and dry thy tears, Pamina,
Dear child, thou hast no need to tell me;
I know the secrets of thy heart;
I know to whom thy love is given.
Fear not, to love I'll ne'er compel thee;
Yet 'tis too soon to set thee free.

PAM.   I hear a voice that calls me hence:
               It is my mother's—

SAR.   Think of her no more.
               Thy life were wreck'd for evermore
               If I to her should once resign thee.

PAM.   How could I e'er forget my mother?
               She loves me—

SAR.   Name her not to me.
               A man to guide thy steps thou needest,
               Since ne'er alone can woman find
               The hidden road that leads to wisdom.

               Enter MONOSTATOS *dragging on* TAMINO.

MON.   So please your highness, come this way;
               Perhaps Sarastro thou'lt obey.

               TAMINO *and* PAMINA *rush into each other's arms.*

PAM.   At last!

TAM.   At last!

PAM.   My love, 'tis he!

TAM.   At last!

PAM.   At last!

TAM.   My love, 'tis she!

BOTH.   At last I see thee face to face,
               And fold thee in my fond embrace.

CHORUS. Who is the stranger?

               MONOSTATOS *separates* TAMINO *and* PAMINA.

MON.   Ha! what effrontery!
               'Tis past endurance, as you shall learn.
                     Kneeling to SARASTRO.

               Behold thy slave before thee kneeling,
               A vile conspiracy revealing;

Was ever tale so shameless heard?
The wretches there—one's half a bird—
Had made a plot to steal Pamina
And run away, had I not seen her.
Thou know'st me, know'st my watchful eye—

SAR. As thou deserv'st I rate thee high.
Thy due reward thou now shalt have.

MON. Too generous art thou to thy slave.

SAR. Then taste a sound bastinado, knave!

MON. Not that I hoped, my gracious lord.

SAR. Enough! it is thy due reward.

MONOSTATOS *is led away by slaves.*

CHORUS. We hail thee, Sarastro, of sages the wisest;
The just thou protectest, the unjust chastisest.

SAR. We bid these strangers welcome here,
If they our holy life would know;
Place then the veil upon their heads,
They must probation undergo.

CHORUS. Sarastro! lead us on, we pray,
The truth to seek with open eyes;
'Tis Nature first that points the way,
Then Reason's laws we must obey,
Thus Wisdom on our souls shall rise.
So cast we off the shades of night,
And ever strive to seek the light.

TAMINO *and* PAPAGENO *are veiled by two Priests
and conducted into the lower temple.*

END OF ACT I

The mind is affected and agitated in death, just as it is in initiation into the Great Mysteries. The first stage is nothing but errors and uncertainties, labourings, wanderings and darkness. And now, arrived on the verge of death and initiation, everything wears a dreadful aspect; it is all horror, trembling and affrightment. But this scene once over, a miraculous and divine light greets the neophyte: he is received into pure regions and meadows, wherein are songs and dances and the solemnity of holy sounds and sacred visions. Here, perfect and initiated, he is free; crowned and devoid of care, he walks in the company of the blessed.

PLUTARCH (?)

ACT II

Scene I

No. 9. March

*Enter the Priests from above, carrying trumpets,
followed by* SARASTRO.

SAR. Brother initiates of the holy mysteries, I have called
you here that you may prepare to receive a new comer.
The Prince Tamino waits at the northern gate of our
temple, full of virtuous desire for that which we too
have sought with toil and patience. Let it be our duty
to watch over him, and hold out to him the hand of
friendship.

1ST PRIEST. Is he virtuous?

SAR. He is virtuous.

2ND PRIEST. Can he be silent?

SAR. He can.

3RD PRIEST. Does he love his fellow men?

SAR. Yes. If you account him worthy, give the sign.
(*They blow their trumpets.*) For him have the gods
chosen out the gentle and virtuous Pamina; it was for
that reason that I removed her by force from her
mother's keeping. That evil woman vaunts her power;
she thinks to dazzle and delude the people with her
degraded superstitions, and utterly to destroy this our
temple of Nature, Reason, and Wisdom. Shall she
accomplish this? No! Let Tamino then be initiated
into our mysteries, and united with her daughter
Pamina, that they may disperse the darkness of super-
stition, and uphold with us the cause of truth and light.

The Priests blow their trumpets.

1ST PRIEST. Great Sarastro, we hear thy words of wisdom, and revere them. Yet, will Tamino have strength to endure the ordeals that await him? Remember, he is of royal blood.

SAR. He is a man; that is enough.

1ST PRIEST. He is young; what if he pay for his initiation with his death?

SAR. He will be in the hands of Osiris and Isis, and will know the joys of the gods sooner than we ourselves. (*The Priests blow their trumpets.*) Lead Tamino and his companion into the forecourt of the temple. And thou, friend (*to the Orator*), fulfil thy sacred duty, and teach them the way of wisdom.

No. 10. Aria

SAR.   Oh hear us, Isis and Osiris!
         For these that seek your light we pray,
         In all their perils grant them patience,
         And lead them safe in wisdom's way.

PRIESTS. Oh lead them safe in wisdom's way!

SAR.   Let them draw near without denial;
         Or if too frail to stand their trial,
         Their youthful ardour call to mind,
         So may they life eternal find.

PRIESTS. So may they life eternal find!

Scene II

Stage dark. Enter TAMINO, *followed by* PAPAGENO.
Distant thunder.

TAM. What a horrible night! Papageno, are you there?

PAP. To be sure I am.

TAM. Where are we now, I wonder?

PAP. Where? If it were not so dark I might be able to tell you. (*Thunder.*) Oh—oh!

TAM. Are you afraid?

PAP. No—not afraid—but I feel a shiver all down my back. (*Thunder.*) Oh—oh!

TAM. What ails you?

PAP. I think it's a fever coming on.

TAM. For shame, Papageno, be a man.   *Thunder.*

PAP. Oh—oh—oh!

Enter Two Priests, with lights.

IST PRIEST. Ye strangers, what has led you to penetrate within our walls? What is it that you seek of us?

TAM. Friendship and love.

IST PRIEST (*to* TAMINO). Art thou ready to fight for these with thy life?

TAM. Yes.

IST PRIEST. Even to die in the attempt?

TAM. Yes.

IST PRIEST. Prince, there is yet time to turn back. One step farther and it is too late.

TAM. I seek the goal of wisdom, and may Pamina's love be my reward.

IST PRIEST. Thou wilt submit to every ordeal?

TAM. Yes, to all.

IST PRIEST. Thy hand upon it!

2ND PRIEST (*to* PAPAGENO). And wouldst thou also seek the goal of wisdom?

25

PAP. Wisdom? No; I'm a child of nature. All I want is to eat, drink, and sleep—and if I could find a little wife too—

2ND PRIEST. That thou wilt never obtain, unless thou submit to our ordeals, and art ready to risk thy life.

PAP. Then I'll remain single.

2ND PRIEST. But if Sarastro had chosen a wife for thee, young and fair, feathered like thyself?

PAP. What is her name?

2ND PRIEST. Papagena.

PAP. Pa—papagena? Well, I should like to have a sight of her.

2ND PRIEST. So thou shalt.

PAP. But when I have seen her, shall I have to die? (*The Priest makes an ambiguous gesture.*) No, I'll remain single.

2ND PRIEST. Thou shalt see her; but thou must speak never a word with her until the appointed time. Canst hold thy peace so long?

PAP. Ay, that I can.

2ND PRIEST. Thy hand upon it.

1ST PRIEST (*to* TAMINO). Prince, the same law of silence is laid upon thee. Thou shalt see Pamina, but thou shalt not speak with her, or with any woman. (*To both.*) This is the beginning of your probation.

No. 11. Duet

TWO PRIESTS

Beware the wiles of woman's weaving,
  Would ye be worthy of this place;
Too many yield to their deceiving,
  And, careless, fall from wisdom's grace.

At last the truth they are perceiving;
　　With scorn requited is their faith.
Too late! their error's past retrieving;
　　What is their end? despair and death.
　　　　　　　　　　　　　Exeunt Two Priests.

PAP. Ho there! bring lights, bring lights! Why are we
always left in darkness?

TAM. Bear thy trial with patience. Remember, it is the
will of the gods.

Enter the Three Ladies.

No. 12. QUINTET

LADIES.　　　　Why, oh why
　　　　　　Did you come to this fell place?
　　　　　　　Fly, oh fly,
　　　　　　Or your steps you'll ne'er retrace.
　　　　　Tamino, this is thy undoing,
　　　　　Soon thou thy folly wilt be rueing.

PAP.　　No, no, what was that I heard?

TAM.　　Papageno, not a word!
　　　　Wilt so soon thine oath be breaking,
　　　　Ne'er with woman to be speaking?

PAP.　　For us some dreadful fate's in store.

TAM.　　Hush, I tell thee, speak no more.

PAP.　　Hush indeed, and speak no more!
　　　　Was ever man so plagu'd before?

LADIES.　The Queen knows all and yet may save,
　　　　But not if you her anger brave.

PAP.　　The Queen? she too is in this place?

27

TAM.   Hush, I tell thee, hold thy peace,
         Wilt the lesson ne'er be learning
         Of the priests' mysterious warning?

LADIES. Dost thou not know what must befall thee?
             Hast thou forgot the Queen's command?
         Hast thou not heard what folk are saying
             About this temple's wicked band?

TAM.   A wise man walks in reason's way,
         Nor cares what foolish folk may say.

LADIES. Who joins their band, we know full well,
         Is damn'd to everlasting Hell.

PAP.   Oh this is really too infernal!
         Must we go to fire eternal
             Down below?
         Tell me, Tamino, is that so?

TAM.   'Tis just what foolish women say,
         And those that fear the light of day.

PAP.   But 'tis the Queen who says 'tis true.

TAM.   Is not the Queen a woman too?
         Have done, and trust to none but me;
         Think on thine oath, and silent be.

LADIES. So stern, so proud, so staunch to duty?
         And Papageno deaf to beauty?

PAP.   If I could only say—

TAM.   Hush!

PAP.   You see my tongue is tied—

TAM.   Hush!

PAP. ⎫
TAM. ⎭   In truth $^{my}_{thy}$ chatter has no ending,

         $^{My}_{Thy}$ tongue is wagging night and day.

LADIES.   We must with shame be homeward wending,
          Since not one word to us they'll say.

ALL.   A man's resolve $^{we}_{they}$ cannot shake
          Who always thinks before he'll speak

PRIESTS (*behind*). What women are those who revile us?
          To Hell with them all, they defile us!

LADIES.   Away! away! away!   *They disappear.*

PAP.   Alack, alack-a-day!   *He falls to the ground.*

          Re-enter the Two Priests.

1ST PRIEST. Prince, thou hast shown thyself a true man.
          Come, yet another journey lies before thee.

          He throws a veil over TAMINO's *head and leads him
          out.*

2ND PRIEST (*to* PAPAGENO). Up, friend, take heart and
          come with me.

PAP.   What? More journeys? I think Papagena will be
          an old woman before I come to the end of them.

          The Priest veils him and leads him away.

Scene III

PAMINA *discovered lying asleep.* MONOSTATOS *steals in.*

MON.   Ha! there's the disdainful beauty. And it was on
          her account that I was beaten! (*He comes closer.*) How
          white she looks! Ah, I've a flaming furnace inside me.
          Is it safe? Ah, just one little kiss would be something
          at least.

No. 13. ARIA

MONOSTATOS

All with passion's fever tingle,
　　Snatch a kiss and give it back;
Then must I alone be single,
　　Just because my face is black?

Love, indeed! can I not feel it?
　　I am man enough, I'm sure!
If I always must conceal it,
　　That is more than I'll endure.

Then my pleasures I'll be taking,
　　No temptation I'll resist;
Laws were only made for breaking—
　　Some one really must be kiss'd!

Now's the time, there's no one looking—
　　Moon, you dare to play the spy?
If you think it's all too shocking,
　　You should shut your silly eye.

He comes close up to PAMINA. *The* QUEEN OF NIGHT *enters from behind.*

QUEEN. Avaunt!   MONOSTATOS *starts back.*

PAM. Mother!

MON. (*aside*). Mother? That must be the Queen of Night.
　　　　　　　　　　　　　　　　　　　　He hides.

QUEEN. Child, where is the young Prince whom I sent to find thee?

PAM. He has joined the initiates of the temple.

QUEEN. Then thou art lost to me for ever.

PAM. No, no, Mother, let us fly this place together, at once.

30

QUEEN. 'Tis useless. My power came to an end when thy
Father died, after handing over to Sarastro the seven-
fold Shield of the Sun. There is but one chance. Take
this dagger: thou shalt kill Sarastro, and bring the
Shield of the Sun to me.

PAM. But, Mother—

QUEEN. Not a word!

No. 14. Aria

QUEEN OF NIGHT

I'll have revenge, no longer can I bear it;
   Hell has no torture I have not endur'd;
Dar'st thou refuse, by all the gods I swear it,
   Thou as my daughter art for e'er abjur'd.

No time for tender yearning,
Such foolish thoughts be spurning!
The fires within me burning
   Consume each vital part.
To hatred and to vengeance they are turning
   What was once a mother's heart.

Yes, 'tis thou shalt strike the fatal blow,
By this thy hand Sarastro's might shall crumble!
   Now, tyrant, tremble!
   Gods, record my vow!   *She disappears.*

PAM. Kill Sarastro? I cannot, I cannot—
   MONOSTATOS *has crept up behind her, and seizes her
   suddenly by the wrists.*
   Ah!

MON. I have heard all. There is but one way to save
thyself and thy mother from Sarastro's wrath.

PAM. What is it?

MON. Be mine!

PAM. Never!

MON. No? Then die! (SARASTRO *has entered from above, and comes up behind them just in time to hurl* MONOSTATOS *to the ground*.) Sir, I am innocent. She would have taken thy life, if I had not been just in time to prevent it.

SAR. Thy soul is as black as thy face. Go!

MON. (*aside—going*). If I can't have the girl, I'll try my luck with the mother.

PAM. Sir, spare my mother. Her grief at losing me has driven her distracted.

SAR. I know all. Thou wilt see how I revenge myself upon her.

No. 15. ARIA

SARASTRO

We know no thought of vengeance
 Within these temple walls,
Where love leads back to duty
 Whoe'er from duty falls;
By friendship's kindly hand held fast,
He finds the land of light at last.
Here each to every other
 By mutual love is bound;
Where every wrong finds pardon,
 No traitor e'er is found.
Those whom this bond can not unite
Are all unworthy of the light.

SCENE IV

TAMINO *and* PAPAGENO *are led in by Two Priests.*

1ST PRIEST. You are to remain here alone. When the trumpets sound, proceed that way. Prince, farewell. Once more, remember: Silence!

2ND PRIEST. Papageno, he that breaks silence in this place, is struck down by lightning. Farewell.

Exeunt Priests.

PAP. Tamino!

TAM. Sh!

PAP. This is a merry life! I wish I were out in the woods again, to hear the birds sing.

TAM. Sh!

PAP. I suppose I may talk to myself!

TAM. Sh!

PAP. (*sings*). La, la, la! Not so much as a drop of water to be had here, let alone anything else.

An ugly old woman enters with a cup of water.

PAP. Is that for me?

WOMAN. Yes, love.

PAP. (*looks at her a long time, and drinks*). Water, nothing more or less. Tell me, fair damsel, are all strangers here treated as nobly as this?

WOMAN. To be sure they are, love.

PAP. Then there will be very few that come here.

WOMAN. Yes, very few.

PAP. I thought as much. Sit down here, grandmother, and talk to me. How old are you?

WOMAN. Just eighteen.

PAP. Just eighty?

WOMAN. Just eighteen.

PAP. Ha! ha! Have you got a sweetheart?

WOMAN. To be sure I have.

PAP. And is he as young as you are?

WOMAN. Not quite—he's a little older.

PAP. (*laughs*). And what's his name?

WOMAN. Papageno.

PAP. (*frightened*). Papageno? (*Pause.*) Where is this Papageno of yours?

WOMAN. Why, there.   *Points straight at* PAPAGENO.

PAP. I your sweetheart?

WOMAN. To be sure, love!

PAP. Then who are you?

WOMAN. My name is—
                    Thunder—she hobbles away quickly.

PAP. Oh—oh! (TAMINO *looks at him.*) I'll never speak another word.

Enter the Three Genii carrying a table spread with food and drink, the flute and the bells.

No. 16. TERZETTO

THREE GENII

Before the gates we once did meet you,
    And set your feet in wisdom's way;
Now for the second time we greet you
    Within the temple walls to-day.

Take now the flute and bells to cheer you,
    Good cheer for weary limbs receive;
When for the third time we draw near you,
    Virtue shall perfect joy achieve.

Prince, be thou brave, light thou shalt see;
Thou, Papageno, silent be.   *Exeunt.*

PAP. Tamino! here's something to eat at last. (TAMINO *walks about, playing the flute.*) Well, blow away! I mean to blow my belly out. (*Drinking.*) This is wine for the gods!

Enter PAMINA.

PAM. At last I find thee! I heard the flute and followed the sound. But thou art silent! (TAMINO *turns away.*) Hast thou not a word for Pamina? (*He motions her to go away. She turns to* PAPAGENO.) Papageno, tell me, what ails him? (PAPAGENO, *his mouth full, motions her away.*) You too? Tamino! Tamino! thou lovest me no longer.

No. 17. Aria

PAMINA

Ah, 'tis gone, 'tis gone for ever,
    Happy dream, 'twill ne'er come true;
Ne'er again return to cheer me
    Hours of joy that once I knew.

O Tamino, only hear me!
    Must I suffer thy disdain?
If no longer thou dost love me,
    Only death can end my pain.   *Exit.*

PAP. You see I can keep silence as well as any one. (*Drinks. The trumpets are heard.* TAMINO *signs to him to go.*) Go on then. I'll come directly; haven't I followed you everywhere? (*Trumpets.* TAMINO *pulls his arm.*) But tell me, Tamino, what is to be the end of all this? (TAMINO *points to heaven.*) Ask the gods, must I? (TAMINO *nods.*) Well, they can at least tell us more than we know. (*Trumpets.* TAMINO *drags him across the stage.*) Not so fast, not so fast; we're in time enough to be plucked and roasted!

TAMINO *pulls him out.*

SCENE V

The Priests enter, followed by SARASTRO.

No. 18. CHORUS

PRIESTS

To Isis and Osiris thanks be given!
The clouds of night the rising dawn has riven;
New light upon this noble youth is breaking;
Soon in our midst his place he will be taking.
    From falsehood's taint his mind is free,
    Fullness of light he soon will see.

TAMINO *is led in.*

SAR. Prince, thou hast borne thyself so far with manly composure. There remain yet before thee two paths of danger. If thy heart still beats for Pamina, if thou still hast the desire to reign as a wise king in the appointed time, then may the gods guard thee safe upon thy way! Thy hand! Let Pamina be brought in.

    Exeunt Two Priests, and re-enter with PAMINA, *veiled.*

PAM. Where am I? (*Pause.*) How dreadful is this silence! Tell me where is Tamino?

SAR. He waits to take his last farewell of thee.

PAM. His last farewell? (*The Priests remove her veil.*) Tamino!

She moves towards him; he motions her back.

No. 19. Terzetto

PAM.   And shall I never see thee more?

SAR.   The gods for each have joy in store.

PAM.   My soul is fill'd with nameless terror.

TAM. \
SAR. /   The gods will keep $\frac{me}{him}$ safe from error.

PAM.   Some dreadful danger's yet impending,
         Thy doom some awful death may be.

TAM. \
SAR. /   Whate'er the gods to $\frac{me}{him}$ be sending,

         Their will $\frac{my}{his}$ law shall always be.

PAM.   Oh lovedst thou with my devotion,
         So calm a mien thou could'st not show.

TAM. \
SAR. / $\frac{\text{I feel}}{\text{He feels}}$ no less that sweet emotion,

         And $\frac{am}{is}$ thine own where'er $\frac{I}{he}$ go.

SAR.   The hour is come that bids you sever.

PAM. \
TAM. /   We part, and part perchance for ever.

TAM. \
SAR. /   The hour is come, $\frac{I}{he}$ must away.

PAM.   O cruel hour, canst thou not stay?
         Tamino! Tamino!

SAR.   He must away!

TAM.   I must away!

PAM.   He must away!

PAM.⎱
TAM.⎰   Fare thee well, Tamino, fare thee well.
                    Pamina,

SAR.   Thou must away, the call obey,
        Tamino! Tamino!
        The hour is come, the call obey.

PAM.⎱
TAM.⎰   Blest hours of rapture, ah! return ye never?

SAR.   The call obey that bids you sever.

PAM.⎱
TAM.⎰   Farewell, farewell!

SAR.   Yet not for ever.

Exeunt omnes.

Scene VI

PAP. (*behind*). Tamino! Tamino! (*Enters.*) Have you left me for ever? If I only knew where I was! Tamino! Tamino! Don't desert me this time, and I'll never disobey you again.   *Going.*

A VOICE. Stand back!

PAP. (*starting back*). Oh, oh! which way? which way? If I could only find the door where I came in!

Makes for the opposite side.

ANOTHER VOICE. Stand back!

PAP. No way out, forwards or backwards. I shall have to die of starvation here. It serves me right; why did I ever go with him?

Enter a Priest.

PRIEST. Wretched man, thy punishment should be to wander for ever in the dark passages of the earth. But the gods are merciful, and pardon thee; yet wilt thou never know the joys of the initiated.

38

PAP. Well, there are plenty of men like me. The greatest joy I can think of would be a good cup of wine.

PRIEST. Hast thou no further desires?

PAP. Not at present.

PRIEST. Thou shalt have thy wish.

Exit. A cup is handed in.

PAP. Ha, there's the wine! (*Drinks.*) That's good. Now I'm happy. (*Drinks.*) I feel so strange. There's something I want still—something—what is it, I wonder?

No. 20. Song

PAPAGENO

'Tis love, they say, love only,
  That makes the world go round;
I should not feel so lonely,
  Had I a sweetheart found.

Then life would be nothing but pleasure;
I'd envy no monarch his treasure.
  No need to learn wisdom in there;
  'Twere wisdom enough and to spare.

  'Tis love, they say, love only, &c.

But no, there's not one that will take me,
Contented and happy to make me;
  If none will give ear to my sigh,
  Indeed of despair I shall die.

  'Tis love, they say, love only, &c.

Each day sees me weaker and frailer,
Each day I grow thinner and paler;
  Was e'er such a sickness as this?
  For me there's no cure but a kiss.

The Old Woman enters, dancing and singing.

WOMAN. Here I am, love.

PAP. So *you* have taken pity on me?

WOMAN. Yes, love; and if you'll swear to be true to me all the days of your life, you shall see how tenderly your little wife will love you.

PAP. Oh, you sweet little darling!

WOMAN. Come, give me your hand and promise.

PAP. Not so fast, love; I'll think it over.

WOMAN (*seriously*). Papageno, I warn thee, delay not. Thy hand, at once, or thou art imprisoned here for ever.

PAP. Imprisoned?

WOMAN. Yes; to live on bread and water, and never to see any one again for the rest of thy days.

PAP. For the rest of my days? Well, better an old wife than none at all! There! (*Gives her his hand.*) I'll be true to thee—(*aside*) until I see some one prettier.

WOMAN. Swear it!

PAP. I swear it! (*She is transformed into a young woman, covered with feathers.*) Pa-pa-papagena!

Enter Priest.

PRIEST. Away! He is not yet worthy of thee. (*He drags her out.* PAPAGENO *attempts to follow; the Priest pushes him back.*) Stand back!

Exit Priest with PAPAGENA.

PAP. (*running after them*). Papagena! Papagena!   *Off.*

Scene VII
The Three Genii are discovered.
No. 21. Finale

3 GEN.   The rosy flush that greets us yonder
         Proclaims the rising day;
      Thus foolish fear gives place to wonder,
         When Reason lights the way.

      Rise, rise, glad Sun, and teach creation
      To live serene in contemplation;
      Restore the reign of light and love,
      Make mortal men like gods above.

PAMINA *has entered with wild gestures, carrying*
a dagger.

1ST GEN.   But look, what maid is that, despairing?

2ND, 3RD ⎱ Pamina 'tis!
GEN.   ⎰

1ST GEN.   Our help she's needing.

3 GEN.   For slighted love her heart is bleeding,
      Let us to her be comfort bearing.
      Unhappy child, 'twere sad in truth
      To lose the love of that fair youth.
      She comes; let us remain unseen,
      To watch what this wild air may mean.
                        They draw aside.

PAM.   No other way but this remains,
      To make an end of all my pains.

GEN.   What dreadful words are these we hear?
      Her grief to madness brings her near.

PAM.   O Death, beloved, I am thine;
      Refuse not thou this heart of mine.

GEN.   Ah! 'tis madness in her waking;
            Haste, ere she her life be taking!
                    They advance towards her.
            Dear Pamina, turn this way.

PAM.   Death is welcome, since the day
            When Tamino could forsake me;
            Yet to hate him nought can make me.
                    She shows the dagger.
            This to me my mother gave.

GEN.   Know'st thou what's beyond the grave?

PAM.   Better thus to end my anguish,
            Than in hopeless love to languish;
            Mother! by thy gift I'll die;
            From thy curse I cannot fly.

GEN.   Maiden, come away with us.

PAM.   Ah! my sorrows who can tell?
            False Tamino, fare thee well!
            Yes, Pamina dies for thee;
            Only this can set me free.

*She is about to stab herself, but is prevented by the
Three Genii.*

GEN.   Stay thy hand! what hadst thou done?
            Could he see thee act so madly,
            It would grieve Tamino sadly;
            He loves thee and thee alone.

PAM.   What? in faithful love abiding,
            His desire he could be hiding?
            Turn'd his face from me away,
            To Pamina nought would say?

GEN.   Ask no more, the reason's hidden.
            Now to fetch thee we are bidden;

Soon Tamino thou shalt see,
How he still is true to thee,
Yes, for thee would even die!
Then to him let us away.

PAM.   Lead me on, no longer stay.

ALL.   When love has join'd two hearts for ever,
No power of man those hearts can sever.
Fear they no danger or alarm;
The gods will guard them safe from harm.

The Genii lead PAMINA *away.*

SCENE VIII

*Two Men in armour are seen standing at each side of a
doorway.* TAMINO *is brought in by Priests.*

MEN.   Who treads the path of toil that unto wisdom
leadeth,
His soul the purge of fire and water needeth.
When him the awful fear of death no more can fright,
Then may he rise to gain the sacred height.
There with the enlighten'd shall he take his place,
To know the mystic rite of Isis face to face.

TAM.   The fear of death shall never shake me;
Let me to virtue's path betake me.
The gates of horror open wide,
I'll seek the truth whate'er betide.

PAMINA's voice is heard outside.

PAM.   Tamino, stay! Oh wait for me!

TAM.   Pamina? I heard her calling.

MEN.   Yes, yes, that was Pamina calling.

TAM.⎫
MEN.⎭ At last to follow $\frac{me}{thee}$ she's free;

43

To part ^{us}/_{you} now no fate has power,

Though death await ^{us}/_{you} in this hour.

TAM. To speak with her am I permitted?

MEN. Yes, now to speak art thou permitted.

TAM.⎫
MEN.⎭ ^{Oh joy}/_{Rejoice} to find her once again,

And hand in hand ^{our}/_{your} end attain!
A maid that fears not death's dark night
Is worthy to behold the light.

> PAMINA *is brought in.*

PAM. O found at last! O faithful heart!

TAM. O hope fulfill'd! No more we part.
 Behold the gates of horror,
  Where pain and death abide.

PAM.   E'en in that place of terror
  I ne'er will leave thy side.
  Nay, I'll be guide for thee,
  As love is guide for me;
 What though the path with thorns be strown
 When love's own roses there have blown?
 Then take the magic flute and play;
 Its note gives light on danger's way.
 That flute from mystic tree was carven,
 And round it mighty spells were woven;
 The sacred bough my father tore,
 Nor fear'd the lightnings' thunderous roar.
 Then take the magic flute and play;
 Its note gives light on danger's way.

44

ALL. That sound of magic has the power

To guard ^{us}_{you} safe in death's dread hour.

TAMINO *and* PAMINA *enter the door and are seen to pass through fire.*

PAM.⎫
TAM.⎬ When fires of passion did assail us,
　　　　Unscath'd by scorching flame we stood.
The voice of music will not fail us
　　When sorrow's waters rise in flood.
　　They pass through water. SARASTRO *and the Priests appear above, welcoming them into the temple.*
　　What glorious vision greets our sight!
　　Our eyes behold the Light of Light.

CHORUS. All hail! all hail! O noble hearts,
　　　Your every danger now is o'er;
　　　Isis to you the rite imparts;
　　　Come! open stands the temple door.

TAMINO *and* PAMINA *enter the temple.*

Scene IX

PAPAGENO *enters, carrying a rope with a noose.*

PAP. Papagena! Papagena! Papagena!
Come then, come then, pretty sweetheart!
'Tis useless! Ah! where can I find her?
No man had e'er a fate unkinder.
'Twas chattering all day and night
Lost me the maid, and serve me right.
Yes, ever since I drank that wine,
　Ever since I that maid did see,
'Tis all on fire this heart of mine,
　And very soon mad I shall be.

45

Papagena! dost thou fly me?
Papagena! don't deny me.
All in vain—she will not hear me.
Life has nothing more to cheer me;
Better far it were to die,
Than endure such pain, say I.

Here's a rope my sighs to strangle;
At the end of this I'll dangle.
No more use for me has life
If I cannot find a wife.
Earth, no more shalt thou deceive me;
Since thou ne'er a mate wilt give me,
Then I'll say farewell to thee.
All fair maids, oh think of me!
'Tis not yet too late to save me;
If but one fair maid will have me,
I will die another day.
Here I am, what do you say?

Are you silent, not a word replying?
Must I really then be dying?
Papageno, take the rope!
Die thou must, there's no more hope.

Well, there's still a chance, I'll wait;
I'll count three ere 'tis too late.
       One! two! three!

Not an answer to be heard;
Then I must fulfil my word.
Nothing can me now restrain;
Fare thee well, thou world of pain.

*He prepares to hang himself; the Three Genii enter
and prevent him.*

46

GEN.   Not yet, O Papageno; wait, we pray;
        Thou hast but one life, throw it not away.

PAP.   Your merry jesting pray continue;
        But if you felt that fire within you
        You'd follow pretty maids, like me.

GEN.   Then set the magic bells a-ringing;
        'Tis they thy sweetheart will be bringing.

PAP.   How foolish of me to forget them!
        At once a-jingling let me set them,
        That I my pretty maid may see.
                He plays on the bells. The Genii go out.

       · Magic bells a-ringing,
           Find my sweetheart's ear;
       Lure of laughter flinging,
           Fetch my sweetheart here.
                The Genii return with PAPAGENA.

GEN.   Now turn about and look this way!   *Exeunt.*

HE.   Pa-pa-pa-pa-pa-pagena!

SHE.   Pa-pa-pa-pa-pa-pageno!

HE.   Caught at last, no more I lose thee!

SHE.   Yes, no more shall I refuse thee.

HE.   Thou'lt be mine to thy last feather?

SHE.   Yes, we'll share a cage together.

BOTH.   How delightful it will be,
         Now the time has come for pairing,
         When that greatest joy we're sharing,
           A nest of little birds to see.

HE.   First comes a little Papageno—

SHE.   Next comes a little Papagena—

HE.   Then comes another Papageno—

SHE.   Then comes another Papagena—

BOTH.   Oh where's the nest will e'er contain us,

            With such a crowd of Papagen^a_os

            As we shall some day hope to see?

SCENE X

Before the temple. It is dark; MONOSTATOS *enters stealthily, beckoning on the* QUEEN OF NIGHT *and the Three Ladies.*

MON.   With silent footsteps forward stealing,
            The temple gates we soon shall gain.

QUEEN. ⎱ In darkness our approach concealing,
LADIES. ⎰ We will our just revenge obtain.

MON.   Remember, Queen, thy word, fulfil it;
            Thy child Pamina must-be mine.

QUEEN.   I gave my word; yes, thus I will it:
            My child Pamina shall be thine.

LADIES.   Her child Pamina shall be thine.   *Thunder.*

MON.   What is that noise of distant rumbling,
            That in me wakes a nameless fear?

QUEEN. ⎱ Yes, hark! it fills the soul with trembling,
LADIES. ⎰ As if an earthquake now drew near.

MON.   All in the temple are collected.

QUEEN. ⎱ We'll fall upon them unsuspected;
LADIES. ⎰ We will destroy that impious band
            With fire and sword throughout this land.

MONOSTATOS *and the Ladies kneel before the* QUEEN.

48

LADIES.⎫ O starry Queen of holy night,
MON. ⎭ To thee allegiance true we plight.

> *Thunder.* SARASTRO *appears above.*

QUEEN.⎫ 'Tis shatter'd and broken for ever our power;
LADIES.⎭ To darkness and death are we doom'd from this
> hour!

> *The* QUEEN, *the Ladies, and* MONOSTATOS *disappear.* TAMINO, PAMINA, *the Genii, Priests, and People have followed* SARASTRO *on to the stage, which now becomes light.*

SAR. The sun's golden radiance drives dark night
away;
The kingdom of error to truth yields the day.

CHORUS. Hail, ye souls enlighten'd! once blind, now ye
see;
Thanks to great Osiris! thanks, Isis, to thee!
Through darkness and error they once sought
their way;
Victorious we hail them in triumph to-day.
By Nature directed,
By Reason protected,
The high place of Wisdom now have they
found,
Their faithful companion the flute's magic
sound.
'Twas only the voice of that music had might
To guard them and guide them to Love and to
Light.

THE END

49

PRINTED IN
GREAT BRITAIN
BY
JARROLD AND SONS, LTD.
EMPIRE PRESS
NORWICH